Zoo Babies

Also by WILLIAM BRIDGES

TRUE ZOO STORIES

WILD ANIMALS OF THE WORLD

BIG ZOO

SNAKE HUNTERS' HOLIDAY*
(with Raymond L. Ditmars)

WILD ANIMAL WORLD*
(with Raymond L. Ditmars)

WHAT SNAKE IS THAT?*
(with Roger Conant)

TOCO TOUCAN*

* Out of print

ZOO BABIES

WILLIAM BRIDGES
Curator of Publications
New York Zoological Park

William Morrow & Company
Publishers   New York

For

LYNN FRANCES CLARK

AND

ANDREA LYNN GOOD

Contents

Foreword

Of all the animal stories I know, the best ones are about the baby animals in the Bronx Zoo.

Grown-up animals are like grown-up people in some ways. They don't play and have as much fun as baby animals and children do. They would rather just sit or sleep or eat or walk around quietly.

But the babies are full of bounce and adventure and experiment. They like to *do* things—Josephine mopping the hospital floor, for instance, or Herbert, the baby walrus, being rolled into the water and scrambling out to do it again.

Every year nearly a hundred babies are born in the Bronx Zoo, and it would take a very big book to tell all their stories. But these are my favorites.

W. B.

Dusty Takes a Bath

Dusty, the grizzly bear cub, had never seen a bathtub until he came to the zoo. Out in the Far West, where he was born, little bears go swimming in the cold mountain streams many times a day. But it was very different when he came to the zoo. There were no mountain streams, and at first there was no water at all except in a little dish for him to drink.

One day it rained and some of the rain blew into the big cage where Dusty lived, and made a tiny puddle on the floor. Dusty must have thought that even a bath in a puddle was better than no bath at all, for he lay down in the puddle and tried to take a bath. But it was such a very small puddle that all the water soaked into his long, coarse hair, and the puddle disappeared.

It was lucky for Dusty that while he was trying to take a bath in the puddle, one of the doctors at the zoo happened to see him. "Well, we don't have a bathtub big enough for a grizzly bear cub, but we can give him something better than a rain-water puddle," said the doctor.

So he hunted around until he found a kind of box, or tank, made out of tin. It certainly had not been meant for a grizzly bear cub's bathtub. It had been made in the first place as a swimming pool for a baby duck.

"I wonder if Dusty will know how to use the duck's

bathtub," the doctor said. "He's never in his life seen anything like that with water in it."

But he placed the duck's bathtub in Dusty's cage, anyway, and put just a little bit of water in it—no more, actually, than there had been in the rain-water puddle.

And Dusty knew exactly what to do! He shuffled over to the tin bathtub and sniffed at it with his nose, and scratched at it with his claws, and looked inside and saw the water. Then he climbed right in and sat down—all of him except his foot, which he couldn't quite find room for.

He looked up at the doctor so wistfully—as if to say he wished there were just a *little* more water—that the doctor hurried to bring a hose. He turned it on and the water splashed all over Dusty, and Dusty stood up in his bathtub and let the water pour over him. Then, when the tub was quite full and almost ready to run over, Dusty squirmed and wriggled and shoved until he found how to sit down in one corner of the bathtub with all of him in the water—well, almost all! He never could quite get the toes of one foot under water. But Dusty didn't care. He had a bathtub all his own.

Lucky Little Mambo

Mambo is a baby gorilla that lives in the Bronx Zoo. If you were to go to the zoo today and watch him climbing and swinging and playing, you would never guess that he was once a sad and lonely baby in a far-away village in Africa, with not enough to eat and nobody to play with.

Mambo was born in the jungle in Africa, and when he was only a few weeks old he was captured by a party of hunters. They thought that people in America would pay a great deal of money for a baby gorilla, so they tied his arms and legs with tough vines and carried him back to their village. There they put him in a dark and dirty room. Once a day someone came to the door and opened it just enough to throw some green bananas on the floor for Mambo to eat. Then they shut the door and went away until the next day.

Mambo sat in the dark room all by himself. The green bananas tasted bad, and green bananas are not the right thing for a baby gorilla to eat, anyway. So he grew thinner and thinner, and sadder and sadder.

One day a man from the zoo came to the village, and the people said to him, "Oh, bwana, we have the most beautiful baby gorilla for you. You must give us a great deal of money for him."

The man went to the dark room and threw open

the door to let the sunlight in. The light hurt Mambo's eyes, because he had been in the dark so long, and he covered them up with his hands. When the man saw Mambo do that, he was very angry with the people of the village because they had not been good to the baby gorilla. He gave them some money, though not nearly as much as they wanted, and he took Mambo away. "I am going to take this baby gorilla back to America with me right away and put him in the Animal Hospital in the zoo, so he will get well," he said.

The very next day he put Mambo in an airplane and they flew to New York. They went straight to the Animal Hospital in the zoo, and they were only just in time, because Mambo was very sick. For a long time the doctor did not know whether he would get well or not.

But finally the day came when Mambo could leave the Animal Hospital and go to the Animal Nursery, where he was to stay until he was old enough to live in a fine new building called the Great Apes House, where people could see him.

The day when Mambo went to the Animal Nursery was the day when he began to have fun. The first thing that happened to him was that he was introduced to the other animals in the nursery. There were many tiny monkeys, called marmosets, that were always leaping from one place to another and making shrill, chirping

noises. Mambo liked to touch their soft fur, but they were too small for him to play with. There was a woolly monkey from South America that was always hanging upside down by his tail and making faces at Mambo. He was the first monkey Mambo ever saw that could hang by his tail. There are lots of monkeys in Africa that have long tails, but they can't wrap them around a limb and hang on, the way a woolly monkey from South America can.

The animal Mambo liked best in the nursery was a little black howler monkey called Ugly. Ugly was not very pretty, but he had a cheerful way of squeaking and chattering and making faces. And he was black all over, just like Mambo. As soon as the little gorilla saw Ugly, he put out his hand and stroked the soft fur on the monkey's head. After that, Mambo and Ugly were good friends.

In Africa, nobody had ever given Mambo a bath or brushed his hair, and so his skin was rough and dirty. After he had been introduced to all the animals, the woman who was in charge of the Nursery put Mambo on a clean blanket on top of a table, and she began to stroke his hair with a soft brush. It felt so good that Mambo doubled his arms under him and almost went to sleep.

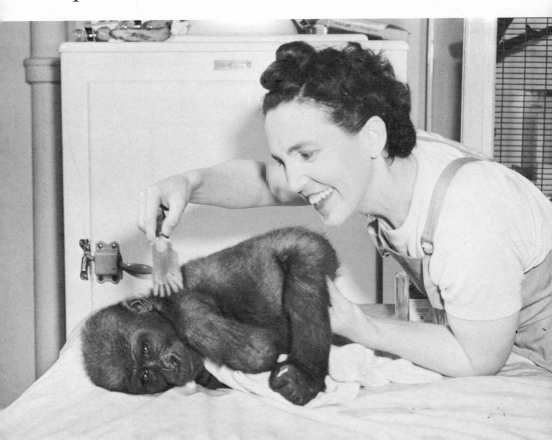

No one ever made Mambo eat green bananas in the Animal Nursery. Instead, every day, after she brushed his hair with the soft brush, the woman took him on her lap and gave him a whole bottle of warm milk. Mambo always drank it as fast as he could and then he had to be burped afterward.

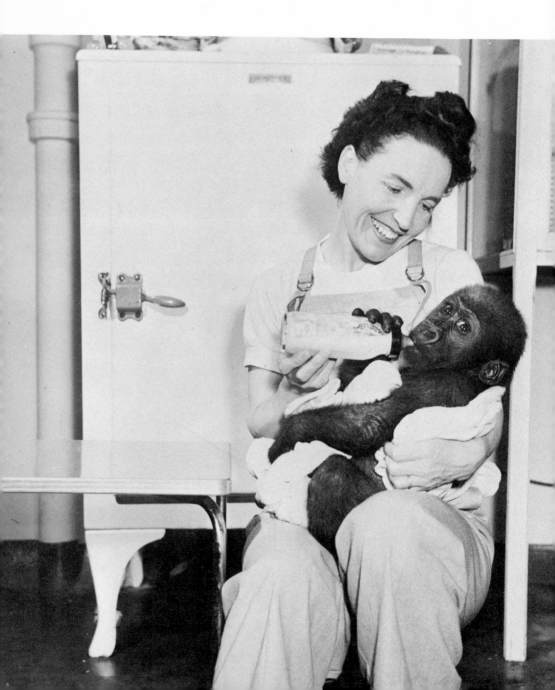

Next he was put on a pair of scales to be weighed. Although Mambo didn't know what a pair of scales was for, and it wasn't as much fun as being brushed or drinking milk, he always sat very still in the basket while he was being weighed.

"Oh, my!" said the woman the first time she weighed Mambo. "You're still a very little gorilla, and you don't weigh as much as you should. We must give you lots of milk to drink, so you'll grow big and strong."

After the weighing it was time for Mambo's rest period in his play pen. But he didn't really rest very

much. He lay on his back and pretended to go to sleep, but as soon as no one was looking he played with the rubber ball in his play pen.

Usually, though, he went to sleep for at least a little while. When he woke up, he was rested and ready to play. Sometimes he made a little tent out of the blanket, or rumpled the blanket all up, or climbed on the sides of the play pen. There were all sorts of things to do.

Mambo was happy in the Animal Nursery and he grew bigger and stronger every day. Soon he forgot all about Africa and how sad and lonely and hungry he had been. He grew fat, and his hair was clean and shining. He was certainly a lucky little gorilla to find such a good home in the zoo.

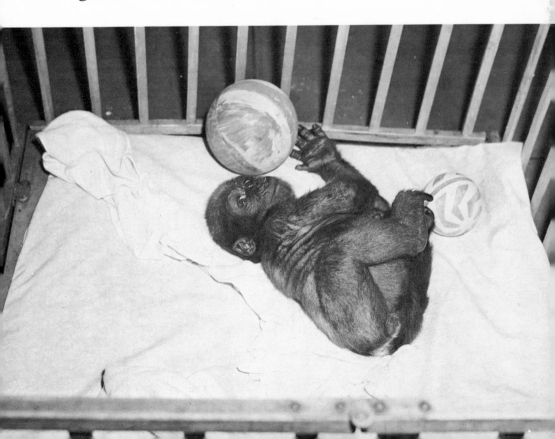

The Panda That Didn't Know About Water

When the people at the zoo decided to build a home for the lesser pandas, they thought of everything these friendly little animals from western China could possibly want.

In China the lesser pandas are called firecats, because they are bright reddish-brown, except for their creamy-white faces and ears and the dark rings around their tails. Firecats can climb a tree as easily as our kind of cat, so the people at the zoo cut down an old tree and set it up in the very large yard where the pandas would live.

Lesser pandas often like to take a nap in a shady place during the day, so the zoo people cut a long piece of hollow log and put it in the yard, too. During the daytime the pandas could go inside the log and sleep. In China the lesser pandas are often found along streams and creeks, so a little creek was made to run through the yard. Finally a man in Florida was paid to send twice a week, by airplane, a great bundle of the special kind of bamboo leaves and stems that lesser pandas like to eat.

When the zoo people had thought of everything and built everything, they tried to get three pandas.

22

They wrote to a man in China asking him to send them three pandas, but he could find only two, so that was all he sent. Luckily, just about that time a baby lesser panda was born in a zoo in California, and when it was old enough to leave its mother it came to the Bronx Zoo in New York.

So the zoo had the three lesser pandas it wanted, and they all lived happily together in the yard. Every day just at noon their keeper brought them all the bamboo they wanted to eat. Almost any time you could see the three little pandas munching bamboo leaves.

The pandas were almost the same age and they were good friends, but there was a difference among them. Two of them had been born in the mountains of western China, and of course they knew all about climbing trees, and sleeping in hollow logs, and jumping across little creeks without getting wet. Those were things that they had learned from their fathers and mothers in the mountains.

But the little panda that had been born in the zoo in California did not know how pandas live in China. All he knew was how his father and mother lived in the zoo. It is true that there was a tree in his yard in California, and he had sometimes climbed it with his mother. And there was a box that his father and mother went into when they wanted to take a nap. But the little California panda had never in his life seen a creek or a pond or any other kind of water, except rain and the small amount of water in the drinking dish in his yard. So naturally he did not know that the stream in the panda yard in the zoo had water in it, or that the water was deep, or that if he fell in he would get wet.

One day after the three pandas had eaten their lunch of bamboo leaves, the two that had been born in China climbed to the top of the dead tree in their yard. There were plenty of branches where they could sit or climb up and down.

But the little panda from California decided to go exploring. He walked from one side of his yard to the other and back again. He walked through the hollow log and then jumped over it. He started to climb the tree and then decided to see what was in the front part of the yard. That was where the little creek was.

When the panda came to the edge of the creek,

he stopped and looked down, for the water did not look exactly like the earth and the rocks and the cement he had been walking on. Still, it looked smooth enough and interesting enough to investigate. So the panda simply walked over the rock at the edge of the water and stepped onto the water. And down he went!

Well! I don't suppose there was ever a lesser panda that was more surprised than this one. He could swim, of course. Even though lesser pandas have never seen water, they can swim without being taught. So he swam to the rocky bank and scrambled onto the rocks. He shook himself all over, and then he shook each of his legs and his head separately, trying to get the water out of his long fur. He had swallowed some of the water, so he coughed and spluttered and shook himself again and again.

It was a lucky thing for him that the keeper happened to come around just then. He saw what had happened, and he quickly got a warm towel and rubbed the little panda until his fur was dry again. Then he put the panda in a small shelter house with an electric heater to make him thoroughly warm and dry so he wouldn't catch cold.

After that, whenever the pandas went exploring in their yard, the one from California always stayed far away from the creek, for he had learned about water.

How Spotsy Was Rescued

For several days after Spotsy was born, nobody knew anything about it except his mother. Spotsy was a Chinese water deer fawn, and he was so small that he could hide quite easily under a burdock leaf or behind a stone. There were several clumps of tall grass in the zoo field where Spotsy was born, and his mother hid him in one of them. He lay so still, and his rusty-brown color was so much like the color of the grass, that even the keeper of the Chinese water deer did not know that he was there.

One day he found out, because Spotsy disobeyed his mother. And if the keeper had not found Spotsy just when he did, the fawn might have been hurt.

This is the way it happened. For several days after he was born, Spotsy lay in the tall grass and did not

think of getting up on his little legs and walking away. His mother was never far away, and now and then she came and nuzzled him with her nose or licked his coarse hair to make it lie smooth.

But after a few days Spotsy began to be restless. He was old enough and strong enough to walk now, and so he began to get up and move away when his mother came to see him. After she had pushed him back in the grass once or twice, Spotsy did something different the next time she came to see him. He waited until she was out of sight, and then he got up and walked in the opposite direction.

Pretty soon he came to a fence. It was a wire fence with fairly large openings between the wires. They were not large enough to let Spotsy's mother go through the fence, even though a full-grown Chinese water deer is nowhere near as large as a shepherd dog. But the openings in the fence were not small enough to keep Spotsy from going through. He put his head and one leg through, and then another fore-leg, and then his tiny spotted body, and then his hind legs — and there he was, on the other side.

Spotsy did not know that deer of another kind lived in the field beyond the fence, and they were dangerous deer. If they saw him, they might very likely trample him with their sharp hoofs and strike him with their antlers. Spotsy kept on walking. He saw the

other deer in the middle of the field and he walked toward them. Because he was so tiny, they did not see him.

Spotsy's mother soon discovered that he had escaped. She ran around the field looking for him, and in a moment she spied him walking across the field toward the dangerous deer. If she could have gone to Spotsy, she could have made him turn around and go back through the fence to safety. But since she was too large to crawl through the openings in the fence, all she could do was to stand and look at Spotsy walking toward danger.

Just then the keeper of the Chinese water deer came along with a bucket of grain for them. He did not know that Spotsy had been born several days before, but he saw Spotsy's mother acting very queerly. Instead of coming to meet him, as she had always done when he brought a bucket of grain, she was running along the fence and looking at something on the other side.

The keeper looked too, and then he saw Spotsy. In just another minute Spotsy would walk out from the tall grass and weeds, and the dangerous deer would be sure to see him. The keeper thought very fast. He ran to the door of the little house where the dangerous deer always came to get their food, and he banged the bucket of grain against the side of the house to attract their attention and let them know that food was ready. As soon as they heard the sound of the bucket, they started toward the house. And as soon as they were in the house, the keeper shut the door and locked them all inside.

Now it was safe for him to run out into the field and get Spotsy. He did not want to frighten the little deer, so he knelt down and held out his hand. Spotsy wondered what it was and came slowly up to sniff. The keeper put his hand around Spotsy and drew him closer. Finally he picked him up and carried him back to the field where his mother was waiting.

But before the keeper let Spotsy join his mother, he got a long roll of chicken wire and tied it around the bottom of the fence between Spotsy and the dan-

gerous deer. The openings in the chicken wire were so small that nothing but a mouse could squeeze through them. And since Spotsy, even though he was very tiny, was bigger than a mouse, he would not get out again and have to be rescued.

How Andy Cut His Foot

Andy the orangutan always wanted to know about everything. When he was very little, he lived in a cage in the zoo's Animal Hospital. Every morning the keeper unlocked the door and held out his arms. Andy climbed into the keeper's arms, and then he put the keeper's necktie in his mouth. He wanted to know what it tasted like.

Next he put his long brown fingers in the keeper's pockets. He wanted to find out if there was anything for him to eat. Almost every morning there was a grape in each pocket, and Andy pulled them out and ate them.

If he was allowed to play by himself, he always climbed up on the pantry shelves and picked up the jars of food. He wanted to know whether they were something to play with. When it was time for him to go back to his cage, he watched very carefully when the keeper put the padlock on the door. Every single time Andy would poke his fingers through the wire at the front of the cage and push the padlock until it went *tink-tink* against the iron bars.

One night when it was time for the people to go home and the animals to go to sleep, the keeper put Andy in his cage and put the padlock on the door, just as he did every night. After he had gone home, and the Animal Hospital was dark and silent, Andy poked his fingers through the wire and pushed the padlock. It went *tink* just once, and then it fell off the door and went *tunk* on the floor.

Andy was surprised, because that had never happened before. This time, when the keeper squeezed the padlock to lock it, he had not squeezed it quite hard enough to make it lock. And so it came unlocked and fell off when Andy pushed it.

Andy sat very still for a moment to find out if the padlock would say anything except *tunk*. It did not say anything at all, so he gently pushed the door

of his cage. And it opened! Very slowly and carefully, in the dark hospital, Andy climbed out of his cage.

In the daytime he had often played in the halls and in the rooms, but there was always someone there to say, "No! No! Mustn't touch!" when he wanted to play with things that were bad for him. Now there was no one in the hospital except some lively little scampering and squeaking white mice that lived in a box across the hall.

Andy heard them scampering and squeaking and he wanted to know what they were doing, so he went over and lifted the top of their box to look in. And all the mice scampered out and away, every one of them still squeaking.

Andy wanted to play with the mice, so he started to follow them. He turned the corner, and there he was in a room full of tables. Naturally he had to find out what was on the tables, so he climbed up on one of them and found that it was covered with bottles. It was so dark that he could not see them very well, and every time he moved a bottle fell off and went *crash* on the hard floor and broke into a thousand little pieces.

That was how it happened that Andy cut his foot. For when he climbed down from the top of the table, he stepped on a piece of glass. It made a sharp little cut in his big brown foot, just under his toes. It did

35

not hurt very much, however, and Andy did not let a little thing like that bother him. He went all through the hospital having fun. He pulled out drawers and scattered papers on the floor. He pulled all the books off the shelves. He found a banana on a table and ate it. Finally, just when he was getting a little tired and sleepy, he found a room he remembered very well, because it was the room where he had his bath every day. So he climbed into the sink and went to sleep.

The next morning there was a great deal of excitement when the doctor came to the hospital. At first he thought a robber had stolen the white mice, but as soon as he saw Andy asleep in the sink he knew what had happened. He did not scold Andy, for he knew

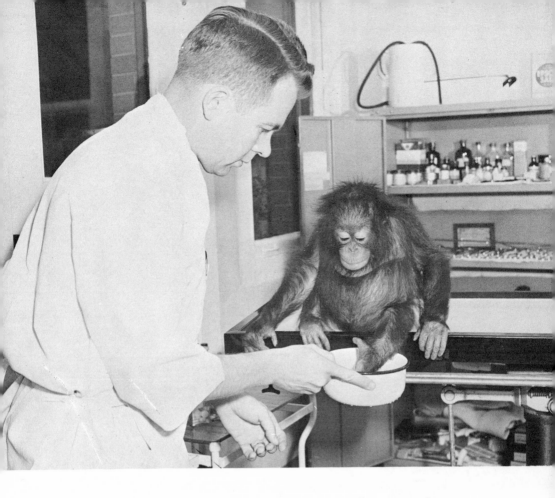

the little orangutan had not meant to do any harm. Instead, the doctor examined him very carefully to make sure he had not hurt himself. That was when he found the place on Andy's foot where the glass had cut him.

"Poor Andy!" he said. "We must put a bandage on his foot."

He carried Andy into another room and put him on a table. The cut place was beginning to hurt a little now, and Andy put his toe in his mouth to make it feel better. Orangutans can put their toes in their mouths very easily.

"I know a quicker way to make it feel better," said the doctor. He brought a pan of warm water and showed Andy how to put his foot in it. That made the hurt go away.

Next the doctor put some salve on the cut place, and then he wrapped a clean white bandage all around Andy's foot. Andy was so interested in everything that he picked up the scissors and pretended to help the doctor cut the bandage to the right length.

"There!" said the doctor. "You are going to be all right now, and your foot won't hurt any more. Now you must go back to your cage, and you mustn't get out at night again."

He carried Andy back to the cage and shut the door. Then he put the padlock on it, and he squeezed it three times to make sure it really was locked.

This time Andy did not put his fingers through the wire to make the padlock go *tink-tink*. He had found something a great deal more interesting to do. He found the end of the bandage, and as soon as the doctor was out of sight he unwrapped the whole bandage and used it to play with!

How Andy Hid Himself in a Sack

When Andy the orangutan went to live in the Bronx Zoo, he had all sorts of things to play with. There was a rubber ball he could bounce and roll, a rope he could climb, and a trapeze he could swing on. But nobody thought that the thing he would like best would be an ordinary old sack.

One day the keeper was cleaning the floor in the big room where Andy lived, and he happened to take a sack along to pick up the banana skins and carrot tops and other things that were left over after Andy's dinner. He dropped the sack on the floor, took his broom, and began to sweep.

That was when Andy got his chance! He picked up the sack and, quick as a flash, he ran over to the other side of the room and began to play with it. First he held it over his head, like a tent. It was quite

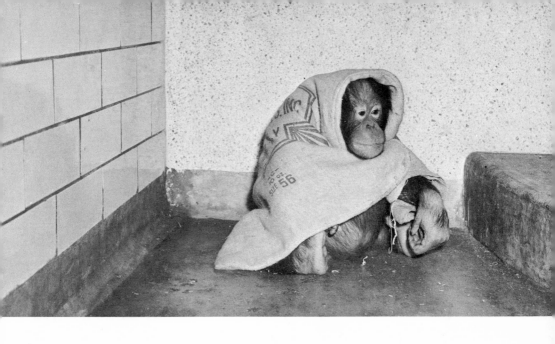

a big sack, and it was thick and warm, so Andy put it over his shoulders. It felt so good that he put it all the way around him and hugged it closer until only his face was peering out. His face and his feet were almost all you could see.

And then, quite by accident, Andy discovered that the sack had a hole in one end. So he pulled it over him, just like a shirt!

How Candy Got Her Name

When Candy the baby elephant came to the zoo, she did not have a name.

"Let's wait and see whether we like her before we give her a name," the zoo people said. "Maybe she won't be a good elephant, and we will have to send her away after a week or two."

So at first they just called her the baby elephant. This is the story of how they happened to name her Candy.

The baby elephant came to the zoo in a huge gray truck with a special door on one side. There was a

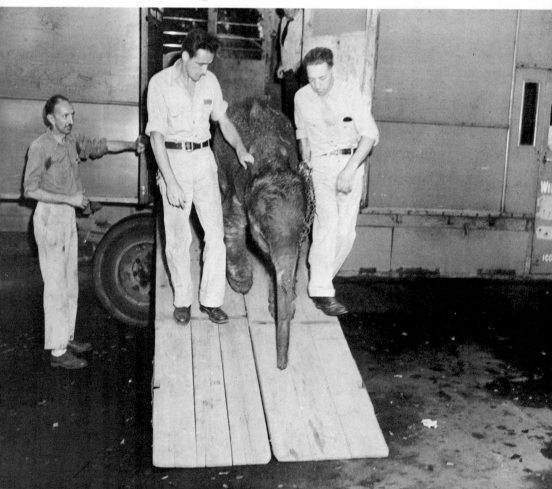

little hole in the door, but it was too high for her to look out of. She could put her trunk through the hole, though, and wave it as if she were waving hello to the people and the other animals. So she rode through the zoo in the truck, waving hello all the way.

When the truck stopped in front of the building where the baby elephant was going to live, the zoo people were a little worried. They knew the only way she could get out of the truck was to walk down some planks that sloped quite steeply from the door of the truck to the ground. And they knew that elephants do not like to walk on anything that sways and springs, for fear it might break under their great weight. They thought that perhaps the baby elephant would be frightened and might even refuse to walk down the planks.

But the instant the planks were put in place and the door was opened, the baby elephant stepped out and walked right down to the ground, as calmly as you please. That was a good sign that she was going to be the kind of elephant the zoo wanted.

Inside the building there was a big, comfortable stall for the new baby, and plenty of hay and grain and apples and carrots and potatoes for her to eat. She was rather hungry after her trip in the truck, so she ate everything in sight. And that was a lot — nearly twenty pounds of vegetables and fruits! But of

course that is not very much for an elephant, even a baby elephant like this one, for she weighed 752 pounds. And she was only one year old.

After lunch the baby elephant decided to go exploring. It was cool and dark in the building, but the sun was bright and warm out of doors, and the baby walked out into the sunshine with her little gray trunk waving in front of her.

Her keeper was already out in the yard. To teach the baby to come to him when he called, he stood in front of her and held a piece of bread in his fingers. The baby stretched out her trunk as far as it would

stretch, and the keeper walked backward, with the baby following him and trying to reach the bread with her trunk. When she had learned to follow him, he gave her the bread and she seized it in the tip of her trunk and stuffed it in her mouth. Twenty pounds of lunch wasn't nearly enough for her!

The next day her keeper brought more bread. He stood quite near the little elephant and gave her some of the bread. Then he put some of the pieces in his pocket. The baby watched him carefully and then she reached forward with her trunk and found his pocket.

46

She thrust her trunk inside, and the tip of it twisted
and squirmed until she found the bread, and into her
mouth it went.

But bread was just a special treat for the baby, because she had to learn to eat hay, like other elephants.
Hay is very filling, and it is a great deal cheaper than
bread. Every day the keeper carried out a bunch of the
choicest and freshest hay and piled it on the ground.
Then he made little bundles of it for the baby elephant to pick up with her trunk. She was so fond of
her keeper that she took the hay and ate it when he

offered it to her, even though she would rather have had apples and bread.

But the greatest fun the baby and her keeper had was when he gave her a bath. He brought out a bucket of water and placed it beside her. Then he scooped up a handful of water and threw it on her, like a kind of shower bath. She enjoyed the bath so much that she always came running as soon as she saw the bucket. But she did not want to get water in her eyes, so she shut them tight when the keeper splashed water on her.

Finally she got so she would give herself a shower bath. She filled her trunk with water from the bucket and sprayed it over herself. The keeper thought she might spray it on him, but she never did. And even when she sprayed herself, she always shut her eyes.

After a week in the zoo, she had learned to follow the keeper everywhere, and he did not need to tie a rope around the little chain on one of her legs so he could tug at it and tell her which way to turn. She did exactly what he wanted her to do and she kept herself clean with shower baths.

So when, at the end of the first week, the people at the zoo came to the keeper and asked him whether he thought they ought to keep the baby elephant, he said, "Yes!"

"All right," they said. "If we're going to keep her, we'll have to give her a name. What shall it be?"

Everybody thought a long time, and then someone said, "She's so sweet, I think we ought to call her Candy."

So they did, and that is her name to this day.

The White Deer That Wanted To Be Friendly

One day late in the fall, when it was almost dark, some duck hunters were crossing Long Island Sound not many miles from New York City. They were in a small rowboat and were rowing hard in order to get home before night.

"Some kind of an animal is swimming toward the shore," one of the men said. "Let's go see what it is."

They rowed harder, and soon they were gaining on the animal in the water. As they drew near, they saw that it was a deer — but the strangest deer they had ever seen. It was snow-white.

The deer was quite small and seemed to be a baby, a fawn born in the previous spring. It was so tired from its long swim in the cold water that it seemed almost glad when the men rowed alongside and pulled it into the boat. It lay on the bottom of the boat, panting and shivering, and one of the men covered it with his coat. As soon as they reached the shore, the men carried it to a barn and put it in a snug stall on a bed of hay.

The next morning they telephoned the zoo and said the zoo could have the white deer. They told how

51

they had lifted the little animal out of the water, and how tame and gentle it was.

But it was quite different when the zoo men went to the barn to get the deer. Overnight it had rested and had eaten some of the hay, and now it wanted to get away. It was frightened of the men, and of the barn, and of all the strange sights and sounds and smells. When the men from the zoo entered the barn, the deer leaped and ran into the wall. It might have broken its neck if the men had not caught it quickly and put it in a wooden box with padding on the sides.

Although they got the white deer to the zoo safely, their troubles were not over, for it became stronger every day and grew more and more wild. The zoo men knew that it would not be safe to turn the little animal out in the woods with the other deer in the zoo. It would be sure to dash away at the first chance, and it might run into a tree or a fence.

So all winter long they kept the white deer in a little room by itself. Every day, when a keeper quietly brought hay and grain for the deer to eat, he talked to it and tried to make friends with it. Little by little the deer grew less frightened, as it learned that nothing was going to hurt it in the zoo.

When spring came and the other deer were wandering through the large, wooded range in the zoo, the men put the white deer in a crate and carried it down to the middle of the range. They let the crate stand there, with the deer inside it, all day long and all night. Some of the other deer were frightened of the crate, for deer are easily frightened by anything new or strange, and they ran to the far corner of the range; but others were curious and came up to sniff at the crate.

The next day, the men opened the door at the end of the crate. They did not know what would happen when the white deer came out, but they were a little afraid it might start to run and hurt itself. Instead, it bounded out and then stopped suddenly. There was some hay on the ground, and it bent over and nibbled at it. Then, calmly and fearlessly, it walked toward the other deer, which were standing a little way off.

This time it was the other deer that were afraid. They had never seen a white deer before, and although it had the shape of a deer like themselves and walked like one of themselves, its color was all wrong! So when the white deer walked toward them, the others walked away. And when it ran toward them, they ran away.

All day long the white deer followed after the other deer in the herd, trying to be friendly — to play and run and eat with them. But they were so afraid of the

54

white deer that they would have nothing to do with it. Once when it ran around the corner of a shelter house right into the middle of a group, the herd's old buck kicked at it as hard as he could. And then he ran away, with the rest of the herd behind him.

For several days it seemed as if the white deer was not going to succeed in making friends with the other deer. But finally they got used to the strange white creature. One day they let it come close while they fed, and that afternoon they all wandered through the woods together. When it came time for them to lie down and rest, the white deer tucked its legs under its body and rested near a big rock, and three other deer rested among the trees only a few feet away. After that, the white deer and the whole herd were friends.

The Chimpanzee that Mopped the Floor

One day a man was walking through the jungle in Africa and he saw a little black animal running along the path ahead of him. "Why, that looks like a baby chimpanzee!" he said to himself.

He ran to catch up with it and, sure enough, it *was* a baby chimpanzee, all fuzzy-haired and only a few weeks old.

The baby was hungry and frightened, for it was lost and didn't know where to find its father or mother. And since the jungle is very, very big, the man didn't know where to find them either, so he put the baby on his shoulder and started home. All the way the baby chimpanzee rode on the man's shoulder with one arm around his neck and one hand holding on to his hair.

When the man's wife saw the baby, she said, "I am going to name her Josephine, and she can live in our house. She can sleep in the rocking chair on the front porch and play in the yard all day."

So they gave Josephine a bottle of warm milk and put her to bed in the rocking chair. Every day she played in the yard in the hot African sunshine, and she grew bigger and stronger. Sometimes she would go into the house and watch the people as they were sweeping or mopping the floor or making beds or

57

cooking. When she would try to catch the broom, or slide on the wet floor, or climb onto the bed, or taste something that was cooking, the people would say, "No, no, Josephine! Bad girl! You go out and play in the yard."

Finally the people decided to move to another house where there was no room for Josephine, and they wanted to find her a good home. So they sent her to the Bronx Zoo.

It was very different in the zoo from living in a house, and playing in the sunshine all day long, and sleeping in a rocking chair. At first, because there was no room for her anywhere else, she lived in the zoo's Animal Hospital.

Josephine wasn't sick, so she didn't have to stay in a cage and take medicine. Every morning her cage was opened, and she was allowed to play in the hall while the keeper mopped the floor. First he would draw a bucket of warm water, and Josephine would climb up on a stool to watch him when he turned the faucet on. She always jumped when the water went splashing into the bucket. Then she followed him down the hall to the closet to get the mop.

At first she was afraid of the mop, because she had never been allowed to touch one in her home in Africa. After a while she learned that the keeper was not going to send her away or scold her, so she began to try to catch the mop as it went *swish-swish-swish* across the floor. Sometimes she really would catch it, and then she pushed the heavy mop forward and backward, just as if she were trying to help.

"Why don't you give Josephine a mop of her own

and let her mop the floor for you while you do something else?" the doctor asked the keeper one morning. He was only joking, but the keeper thought it would be fun to see what would happen. So he found a short piece of broom handle and tied a rag on the end of it. Then he filled a pan with warm water and put a sponge in it.

"You're my helper, Josephine," he said. "You mop the floors and I'll wash the windows."

That was the first time in her whole life that Jo-

sephine ever had a mop and a pan of water and a sponge to do anything she liked with. First she bent over and tasted the water. Then she tasted the mop. Then she put the mop in the water and got it all wet. Next she squeezed the sponge, the way the keeper always did. And finally, to everybody's surprise, she stood up and swished her own little mop back and forth on the floor!

But I am sorry to say that Josephine didn't do a very good job of mopping the whole floor. She

mopped just one tiny spot, and then she wet the mop
and scrubbed the same spot all over again. At last she
got tired of doing that, so she emptied the water on
the floor and put the pan on her head like a hat.

After that, the keeper didn't tell her she could be his helper any more. He always mopped the floor himself. And when people asked him why he didn't let Josephine help him, he always said to them, "Josephine is the cleanest little chimpanzee I ever saw. When she mops the floor, she uses a whole pan of water for one tiny little spot. I don't let her help me any more because I would have to spend all morning carrying pans of water to her!"

The Baby Walrus and the Game of Roll-Roll-Splash

One morning an expressman came to the gate of the zoo with a big box in his truck. "Here's a box that came to you from Greenland by air express," he said. "It has an animal inside, but I don't know what kind it is."

There was no sign on the box telling what kind of an animal it was, so the people at the zoo tried to look inside. First they saw some gray, wrinkled skin. Then they saw some whiskers. Then they saw a small, twinkly eye. "Why, it's a baby walrus!" they said. "It's just exactly what we want, and we have a wonderful home for him. Take the box to the pool right over there."

They showed the expressman where to put the box and, as quickly as they could, they got a hammer and began to knock the boards off the side so the walrus could come out. As soon as all the boards were off, out rolled the biggest, fattest baby that had ever come to the zoo. He sniffed the air and he looked at the big swimming pool. Then he lifted his flippers and began to drag himself along in the funny, shuffling way that walruses have. He waddled all the way around the bank at the edge of the pool. He seemed to want to know all

about it and where everything was. Or maybe he was looking for fish.

"Of course! He's hungry!" said the people at the zoo. "The poor baby hasn't had anything to eat since he left Greenland yesterday. Quick! Give him a bucket of fish!"

One of the men ran and got a bucket of fish. First he ground it up until it was as fine as hamburger. Next he poured a gallon of milk over the fish, and then a cup of cod-liver oil. When he stirred it all up it did not look very appetizing, but he knew that was the way a baby walrus would like it. He poured the mixed-up fish and milk and cod-liver oil into a dishpan and hurried back to the pool.

When the baby walrus smelled the fish, he could hardly wait. He began to waddle after the man, and he waddled almost as fast as the man could walk. As soon as the pan was on the ground, he put his face right down into it and began to suck up the fish and milk and oil. He didn't look up once. He just kept his whole face in the pan and whooshed the fishy, milky, oily food into his mouth.

When it was almost all gone, he did look up. There was fish and milk and oil all over his face, and in his mouth was the tail of a whole fish—one that had not been ground up like hamburger.

After the baby walrus had licked the dishpan until

there wasn't a drop of fish or milk or cod-liver oil left, he waddled over to the edge of the pool and just rolled in and dived under the water. That washed his face clean, and for the rest of that day he dived and rolled and swam and had fun in the water.

The people at the zoo thought Herbert would be

a good name for the baby walrus, so that was what they called him. Soon he learned to come whenever anyone shouted "Herbert!" He always thought they were bringing him more fish and milk and oil whenever anyone called to him.

In the middle of every morning and in the middle of every afternoon, his keeper brought him a dishpan full of food, and Herbert always ate every drop of it. No wonder he grew fatter every day! He weighed 240 pounds when he came to the zoo, although he was only five months old, and when he was a year old he weighed 512 pounds.

After his breakfast Herbert always took a nap. He stretched out on the rocks at the edge of his pool, crossed his stubby little hind flippers, and shut his eyes. Before you could say "Jack Robinson!" he was asleep. Usually he dreamed while he was asleep, and then he blew hard through his nose and huffed and puffed and flapped his flippers as if he were swimming. Sometimes he made a noise as if he were whooshing fish and milk and oil into his mouth. Eating seemed to be the thing he liked most to do, and he probably dreamed about it.

After the morning nap it was playtime. Herbert and his keeper invented a game called roll-roll-splash. This is the way they played it. First Herbert lay on his side or back, with his flippers in the air. Then the

keeper got behind him and began to push. He had to push very hard, because Herbert was so fat. Herbert started to roll — at first just a little, and then more and more. Over and over he rolled, down the sloping bank toward the edge of the pool. The keeper followed him,

pushing all the time. Then, right at the edge of the pool, he gave one final push — and *splash*, Herbert rolled into the water!

And what a splash he made! Anybody watching him might have thought that all the water would splash out of the pool. But it didn't. The only thing that came out of the pool was Herbert. He always swam to the bank and climbed out and waddled up to his keeper. Then he lay down on his back, ready to start the game of roll-roll-splash all over again!

The Baby Tapir That Ran Away

This is a story about a baby tapir that ran away from his home in the zoo and lived in the dark woods until he got hungry and came home again.

The baby, whose name was Streaky, was born in South America and came to the zoo when he was very little. Even though he was only a few months old, he was strong and could run quite fast. In South America he used to run through the forest and dig up roots and eat leaves, all by himself. But when he came to the zoo, he lived in a big yard with a fence around it so people could see him, and he wasn't allowed to run through the forest any more.

One day the keeper at the zoo accidentally left the gate open, and Streaky ran out of the yard and straight toward a part of the zoo that is all woods and bushes — almost like the forest in South America.

The keeper saw Streaky running toward the forest and he shouted at him. "Hey, Streaky! Come back, Streaky!" he shouted.

But Streaky paid no attention. He kept right on running.

The keeper ran after Streaky, but Streaky could run twice as fast, so pretty soon he reached the woods and ran under a bush where the keeper could not see him.

All morning long Streaky had a wonderful time. It was just like being back in South America. He walked through the cool, dark woods and sniffed the cool air that smelled of leaves and earth and growing things. He came to a little brook that bubbled over the rocks, exactly like a little brook in the forests of South America. Streaky went wading in the brook and got a nice cold drink of water.

But pretty soon it got to be noon, and then it got to be afternoon. The shadows grew longer and longer. Pretty soon it was almost dark and then, after a while, it was really dark.

Streaky began to feel hungry.

Of course, when he had been hungry in South America, there were always plenty of roots and leaves to eat. But Streaky had not found any roots in this forest that smelled good to eat, although he had sniffed at the ground several times. He tasted a few leaves, but they were bitter and not good to eat.

And now it was dark, and a good deal colder than it was at night in South America. Streaky was not afraid of the dark and he had not seen or heard or smelled any animal that might pounce on him and hurt him. So nighttime did not bother him at all. But he was really very hungry.

Well, there was no use worrying about it, so Streaky lay down under a bush, on a little pile of

leaves, and went to sleep. And, like a sensible little tapir, he slept soundly all night long.

But next morning, as soon as it was light, Streaky woke up, and he was even hungrier than he had been the night before. He stood up and looked around and sniffed the air. Something seemed to tell him that if he turned around and went back under the bushes and past the brook and past some more bushes, he would come out of the woods just at the place where he went in. And not far away from there he would find his old home in the zoo, where every morning the keeper brought him a pan of vegetables for breakfast.

So Streaky turned around and went back through the woods. After a very few minutes he passed the brook, and then he passed the bush where he had hid from the keeper, and there, ahead of him, was a path he remembered. Streaky walked out on the path and looked around.

He saw something that looked so good he could hardly wait to reach it. It was a great big pan of bread and bananas and apples and carrots and celery — all the things that Streaky especially liked. And it was sitting right down on the ground, waiting for him to come and eat it.

Streaky ran over to the pan as fast as his little legs could carry him and began to eat. He was so hungry he scattered food all around, but he didn't care.

Pretty soon all the food was gone, and just then the keeper came around the corner. "Why, here's Streaky back home again!" he said. "I *thought* he would come home if I put some food out for him. Come on, Streaky. Let's go back where you belong, so people can see you."

The keeper started toward Streaky, but now Streaky wasn't hungry any more and he thought about the fun he could have in the forest. So he ran away again, right back to the woods! This time, however, he didn't run any farther than the edge of the woods. Perhaps he remembered that even though it was fun to play in the woods, there wasn't anything to eat there. Anyway, he stood at the edge of the woods and looked at the keeper to see what he was going to do.

The keeper did the very best thing he could do. He went and got a bottle of warm milk. He knew that warm milk was the thing Streaky liked more than anything else, and that if anything would make Streaky come back, that was it.

He held out the bottle of warm milk so Streaky could see it, and he walked slowly toward the little tapir, talking to him all the time. "Look, Streaky. Look at the warm milk," he said. "Wouldn't you rather have a bottle of warm milk and plenty to eat every day, instead of running off to the forest and getting cold and hungry?"

Streaky let him walk right up to the edge of the forest beside him. The keeper bent down and gave Streaky the bottle of warm milk, and held it until Streaky drank every drop of it. Then the keeper walked toward the yard and through the open gate, and Streaky trotted along behind him and went back to his home in the zoo. And after that he never ran away again.

The Greatest Acrobat in the Zoo

Of all the animals in the zoo, the best acrobat is the whitehanded gibbon that comes from Malaysia, far over on the other side of the world. It can climb to the top of the tallest tree and jump from one tree to another without falling. It can stand on a slender branch that is swaying in the wind and hold on with its toes while balancing itself with its long arms. A gibbon feels a great deal safer up in a tree than it does on the ground.

One day a baby gibbon was born in the Bronx Zoo. His father and mother lived in the trees growing on a little island and, of course, the baby lived in the trees too. He was not old enough to walk by himself. For many weeks he clung tightly to his mother's soft golden-brown hair, and his mother carried him everywhere.

When the wind blew hard, his mother sat on a small branch in the top of the tree, with her legs doubled up to make a snug lap for her baby, and the little gibbon looked at the other branches swaying in the wind. He was never afraid, for he knew his mother would not fall. Even when his mother was climbing through the trees and could not make a very good lap for her baby, he was not afraid. He clung to her fur no matter what she did.

The baby looked so much like his father that the people in the zoo named him Junior. They said he would grow up to be strong and golden-colored like his father.

If it sometimes seemed dangerous for Junior's mother to run along the branches and leap from one tree to another with Junior clinging to her, there was something else she did that seemed even more dangerous. That was when she climbed a wire that stretched from the ground to the top of one tree. The wire sloped very steeply, but the mother gibbon walked

straight up it, balancing herself with her arms. Junior clung to her and never moved the least little bit, except to turn his head to see where they were going.

All summer long Junior held on to his mother while she climbed and jumped and walked up and down the wire. And then came the day when Junior

was big enough and strong enough to leave his mother and begin to be an acrobat himself. At first his mother did not let him do very many things. If he walked on a branch, she walked close to him so he could reach her hand if he started to fall. But he never even began to fall.

Finally Junior began to play on the wire, but he stayed very close to the trunk of the tree, and his mother always watched from a place where she could help him if he slipped. Sometimes she hung by her long arms from a branch close to the wire while

Junior practiced hanging by one hand and his feet.

Then he got so he could hold on with his feet as well as his hands, for a gibbon has long, strong toes that are almost as good as fingers. By this time he was such a good acrobat that his mother did not have to watch him, and he was allowed to run through the tree and play on the wire all by himself.

The most exciting time of all was when Junior was ready to make his first jump from one tree to another. He was in the top of the tallest tree, and his father and mother were in another tree. Junior wanted to go to them, but he didn't want to climb down to the ground and then climb the other tree, so he got ready to jump. First he walked out on the end of the branch nearest the other tree where his father and mother were. The wind ruffled his fur and the branches swayed gently. Junior took a deep breath and — *whoosh!* Out he went, out and down, his arms outstretched to catch the branch below him on the other tree. And he caught it! It was his very first jump — nearly twenty feet across and down — and he made it just as safely as if he had been jumping from one tree to another all his life.

Junior ran along the branch and huddled up beside his mother. Of course gibbons can't talk, but if they could his mother would have told him that now he was a real acrobat and she wouldn't be worried about him any more.

Junior has grown up now and is as big as his father, although the people in the zoo still call him Junior. And they say he is the greatest acrobat in the zoo.

The Buffalo Calf That Broke His Leg

For a great many years a herd of buffalo lived in the zoo. They were healthy and contented animals, with plenty to eat and a snug shelter house where they could go in winter when the freezing rain fell in stinging pellets all day long. It was far nicer than it used to be on the wide plains of the West where the buffalo had to face the rain and the snow with no protection.

Everybody in the zoo was very proud of the buffalo herd, especially their keeper, whose name was Bill. He said they were the finest buffalo outside the great government reservations in the West, and probably he was right. But there was one thing that bothered him. He wished a baby buffalo would be born, for it had been many years since he had had a buffalo calf to take care of.

Then one spring morning when he went to the buffalo range to give the animals a bale of hay for their breakfast, there, in the middle of the range with its mother, was a stout little buffalo calf. The keeper was so pleased and happy that he dropped the hay and ran all the way back to the center of the zoo to tell the other people that a buffalo calf had been born during the night.

"That is wonderful news," they said. "And because you take care of the buffalo, we will call the calf Billy."

All during the summer the keeper watched over Billy with the greatest of care. He put the calf and his mother in a special part of the buffalo range all by themselves. There they had special food and the choicest hay, and there was no danger that one of the big buffaloes might bump into the baby and perhaps step on it.

But one day something happened. The gate in the fence between Billy and the other buffaloes was not very securely fastened. When the baby butted it with his hard little head it flew open, and Billy ran out into the big field where all the other buffaloes were.

At first they paid no attention to him, because they were busy eating grass. Billy was not in any danger until all of a sudden something frightened the big buffaloes. Perhaps it was an automobile passing on the street not far away; perhaps it was some other sudden noise. Anyway, the buffaloes began to run, and they ran straight toward Billy. They ran right over him.

When the herd had passed, Billy was lying on the ground. He could no longer stand on his four

sturdy legs, for one of them was broken. He lay on the ground a long time. His mother came out of her special pasture and stood over him, nudging him with her nose, urging him to get up. But he could not get up, because his leg was broken.

Several hours later, when it was time for the keeper to bring the hay for the afternoon feeding, he saw that the gate was open and then he saw Billy in the big field. In great fright he ran to see what the matter was. When he saw that Billy's leg was broken, he called the zoo's doctor, and they put the little animal in the ambulance and took him to the Animal Hospital.

It was very hard to hold Billy while they examined his leg and washed it and made a kind of frame out of wire and wood and bandages to hold the bones in place. Billy was frightened and he did not know that the doctor was trying to help him. But after a while the frame was finished, and they fitted it on Billy's leg. The doctor called it a splint. It was just large enough and long enough to hold the broken bones in place and to let Billy stand up and walk while his leg healed.

They took Billy out of doors and let him try to walk. He could walk almost as well as before! He looked rather funny with the great white bandaged splint on his leg, but he could walk.

A few weeks later the broken leg was healed, and they took the splint off. Nobody could possibly tell that Billy had once had a broken leg. He was taken back to the buffalo range, and his mother was glad to see him again. By this time Billy was much larger and stronger and he was allowed to run with the other buffaloes in the herd. He could run as fast as they could now, and they never ran over him again.